5/07

7

D0389879

Cal Ripken, Jr.

Play Ball!

BY **Cal Ripken, Jr.**
and Mike Bryan

Adapted by Gail Herman
Illustrated by Stan Silver

DIAL BOOKS FOR YOUNG READERS
NEW YORK

Dial easy-to-read

For my family, who shows me the way

Published by Dial Books for Young Readers
A division of Penguin Putnam Inc.
345 Hudson Street
New York, New York 10014

Adapted from *The Only Way I Know* by Cal Ripken, Jr., with Mike Bryan, published by Viking Penguin.
Copyright © Cal Ripken, Jr., 1997, 1998.

PHOTOGRAPH CREDITS

Front cover, Cal (Jonathan Eric/Sports Photo Masters); page 1, Cal (Walter Iooss); page 7, Cal running bases (Jerry Wachter Photography); page 9 left, Dad in his early days; page 9 right, Cal with bat and ball; page 10, spring training in Daytona Beach, Florida, from left: Dad, Fred, Mom, Billy, Elly, Cal; page 14, Cal with Little League team; page 18, Cal at age 16 with Dad at Memorial Stadium; page 20 left, Cal receives MVP award in the Caribbean League for the second year in a row; page 20 right, Cal in 1981 with the Rochester Red Wings; page 24, Cal in 1982 (Jerry Wachter Photography); page 27 left, Cal with Ryan in the pool (Walter Iooss); page 27 right, Cal with Rachel at Camden Yards (Jerry Wachter Photography); page 29, Cal with Dad and Billy at Camden Yards (Jerry Wachter Photography); page 30, Cal fielding the ball (Allsport); page 31, Cal missing the ball (Allsport); page 34, Cal running after hitting the ball (Chuck Solomon/*Sports Illustrated*); page 35, Cal (David Liam Kyle/*Sports Illustrated*); page 39, Cal being congratulated by his teammates (Walter Iooss); page 40, Cal hitting a home run on Streak Night (Chuck Solomon/*Sports Illustrated*); page 41, Cal running bases after hitting a home run (John Iacono/*Sports Illustrated*); page 42, Cal being cheered by fans (Walter Iooss); page 43 left, Cal with Eddie Murray (Allsport); page 43 right, Cal gets a kiss from his son, Ryan (Walter Iooss); page 44, Cal with various kids (Allsport); page 45, Cal takes a bow (Walter Iooss); page 46, Cal (Walter Iooss).

All photographs not credited above are courtesy of the Ripken family.

Printed in Hong Kong on acid-free paper

The Dial Easy-to-Read logo is a registered trademark of Dial Books for Young Readers,
a member of Penguin Putnam Inc., ® TM 1,162,718

First Edition

1 3 5 7 9 10 8 6 4 2

LIBRARY OF CONGRESS CATALOGING IN PUBLICATION DATA
Herman, Gail, (date)
Cal Ripken, Jr. : play ball! / by Cal Ripken, Jr., and Mike Bryan ;
adapted by Gail Herman ; illustrated by Stan Silver.
p. cm.
Adaptation of: The only way I know / Cal Ripken, Jr., and Mike Bryan. 1997.
Summary: A simple biography of the highly honored player for the Baltimore Orioles,
who in 1995 broke the record for playing the most games in a row.
ISBN 0-8037-2415-2 (hardcover)
1. Ripken, Cal, 1960–   —Juvenile literature. 2. Baseball players—United States—Biography—
Juvenile literature. 3. Baltimore Orioles (Baseball team)—Juvenile literature.
[1. Ripken, Cal, 1960– . 2. Baseball players.] I. Bryan, Mike. II. Silver, Stan, ill.
III. Ripken, Cal, 1960–   Only way I know. IV. Title.
GV865.R47H47 1999 796.357′092—dc21 [b] 98-26366 CIP AC

Reading Level 2.4

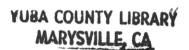

Contents

Play Every Day

The year was 1981. I was sitting on the Orioles bench waiting to play pro baseball.

Me? I thought. Sitting on the bench? I was not used to this. This wasn't what I had in mind. Not for the big leagues.

But the Baltimore Orioles had always been my favorite team. While I was growing up in Maryland in the 1960s and 1970s, they had one winning season after another. By 1981, they had been in five World Series, and they had won two championships.

It was my first year with the Orioles.

How can I break into this lineup? I wondered. And how can I stay there?

I came up with two answers: 1) Play well. 2) Play every day.

I decided to play so well that the manager would have to keep me in the game.

One year later, I broke into the lineup. I remembered those questions, and those answers. Because I worked hard and played every day, I was able to break the record for playing consecutive games. That's one game right after the other. The record was 2,130 games in a row.

I played through some good seasons and some that were not as good. I had hitting streaks and slumps. But I kept going. I kept playing my best. I kept doing my job.

That's what I learned, growing up in the Ripken family.

A Baseball Family

My father began working for the Orioles the year my parents got married. And he worked hard. First he was a player in the minor leagues. Then he was a manager in the minors.

The Orioles had minor league teams all over the country, so my family traveled around a lot.

We had a house in Aberdeen, Maryland, which is where we lived. But during baseball season, we would pack up and go with Dad. All together, my family rented houses in fourteen different towns.

For me, it was just part of growing up in a baseball family. My sister, Elly, is the oldest. I am next, then my brothers, Fred and Billy. Billy is the other baseball player in the family.

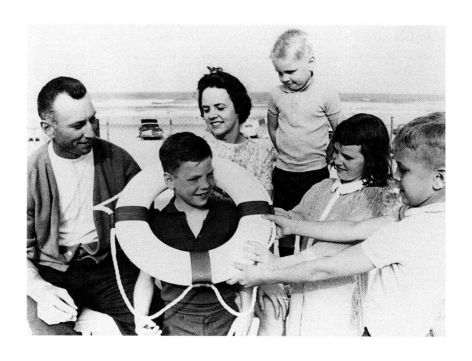

When we were really young—before we went to school—we would travel with Dad to Florida for spring training. We stayed there for four to six weeks at a time. When spring training was over, we'd load up the car and drive to a new town.

Sometimes it was fun. But life on the road could be tough too. It was hard to make friends. We never stayed anywhere long enough, so we looked to one another for friendship.

First grade was hard. I missed my family when I was in school. I wanted to go home. So I would wait for the teacher to be busy. Then I would get my coat and run out the door.

Finally, I settled down. And of course I still played with Elly, Fred, and Billy after school and on weekends.

What did we do? Well, we all grew up with baseballs in our hands. But we also played basketball, football, soccer, and even Ping-Pong. We went bowling too.

I was competitive. And I admit, I cheated. Elly and Fred tried to keep me out of some games. But I would beg to play. As I got older, I learned one thing. To see how good you really are, you have to play by the rules.

Cheating means nothing.

All of us were good at sports. We were also good at breaking windows. The older we got, the more we broke. But Dad didn't get mad unless we played ball indoors. He just taught us how to fix the windows.

As we grew older, we didn't travel as much. Dad was away a lot, and I missed him. Mom had to be both our dad and our mom. She drove us everywhere. She went to all of our Little League games. But Dad was always there when we really needed him.

We spent some summers in Asheville, North Carolina. I spent a lot of time in the park with Dad. I'd hit some balls before games. I'd field some grounders.

I talked to the players. I got tips. I played on a Little League team there too. Baseball became more and more important to me. That's where I put my energy.

And I really started to learn.

The Draft

In 1975, Dad took a job with the Orioles in Baltimore, right near our home. We were all really happy. He would be around more now—even during baseball season.

When I made my high school baseball team, Dad was there. I was only fourteen. I was playing against juniors and seniors. No wonder I only had 4 hits—out of 35 at-bats!

For the first time, I had my dad around to help me. He worked with me on my hitting. He taught me to turn my left shoulder during the pitcher's windup. This helped me time the hit and get my body into the swing.

By the playoffs, I was much better. Playing against older guys was a challenge, but I loved it.

I also loved math. In eleventh grade, I had a math teacher who gave a tough

homework problem every night. There was one girl who got the right answer day after day. But one day, the teacher said that even she would have trouble with this problem.

I saw it as a challenge.

That night I studied all my math books. I worked for hours. I wanted to shout when I got the answer. But I didn't. Everybody was sleeping.

The next day, the teacher asked who solved the problem. The girl did not raise her hand. But I did. The teacher was surprised. I went to the blackboard to show my work. I got the answer right. It was a great moment.

Meanwhile, my game was still improving. Baseball scouts started coming to games when I was seventeen. They were searching for good players.

On the morning of the baseball draft, the day the pro teams choose players, I waited nervously. I wanted to play for the Orioles, of course.

Finally someone brought the news to me in class: The Orioles picked me!

Dad shook my hand. Then I knew it was for real. I was a professional ballplayer!

The Minors

I was finally a pro. But a major leaguer? No way. Like almost everybody else, I had to play in the minor leagues first. I had to develop my skills.

Playing in the minors wasn't at all the way I had pictured it. I felt homesick. In my first game, I made three errors. And I wasn't much better at the plate. It wasn't the best start.

Over the next three years, I got better and better. I learned new skills. My hitting grew stronger too. In the winters, I played

ball in Florida and Puerto Rico. I won my team's trophy for Most Valuable Player twice.

In my last year in the minors, I played in an unbelievable game. It became world-famous, in fact.

The date: April 18, 1981. My team was from Rochester, New York. Our opponents were from Pawtucket, Rhode Island.

Pawtucket tied the game in the bottom of the ninth inning. We kept playing. *Hours*

passed. Finally, we scored again in the twenty-first inning. But so did Pawtucket.

It was late and it was really cold. The wind was blowing. And still we kept playing. It became so cold that someone built a fire in an oil drum.

Finally, the umpires stopped the game in the thirty-second inning. We had played for eight hours and seven minutes.

About two months later, on June 23, we finished the game. Pawtucket won in the bottom of the thirty-third inning. It was the longest game in baseball history.

In August 1981, I was called up to Baltimore. I was entering the big leagues!

The Baltimore Orioles

Now I worked side by side with my dad. He was the third base coach for the Orioles.

I was almost twenty-one. And I was spending all my time on the bench. Waiting.

If I ever get in the lineup, I thought, I'm not coming out.

During the winter, the third baseman was traded to another team. It was my position now.

The next year became my real rookie season. On Opening Day I hit a two-run homer. I thought I had it made. Then I went

into a slump. I couldn't hit a thing.

Later that season, we played a game against Seattle. I was up at bat. I wanted a curve ball. I wanted it so badly, I thought I saw it coming. I waited for the ball to curve.

I waited and waited. Then I realized the ball was never going to curve. It was a fastball. Ninety-four miles per hour.

It clocked me right on the head.

I fell flat on my back. My helmet cracked. I was okay. But I couldn't let anyone think I was scared of the ball. I had to become a better hitter.

Some people think that hit woke me up. Maybe it did, because I broke my slump.

On May 29, 1982, I was not included in the lineup for the second game of a doubleheader. It would be the last time I wasn't in the starting lineup for sixteen years.

That summer the manager switched me to shortstop. It worked out fine. By the end of my first season, I was named Rookie of the Year!

My Family

Could my rookie season have gone better? Maybe if we had won the division championship. . . .

But the very next year, the Orioles won the World Series, and I was named MVP. Most Valuable Player.

The years passed, and the team was feeling good. I met Kelly, the woman I was going to marry.

Now we have two children. Rachel was born in 1989, and Ryan was born in 1993.

I'm a professional ballplayer, and that

means I'm away a lot. But I learned from my dad how to be a good father, even when I'm on the road. So my family is very close.

When I take my children out, I'm just Rachel and Ryan's dad—not Cal Ripken, Jr., baseball player. Kelly and I want our children to have regular childhoods. If our first child

had been a boy, we would have named him Calvin Ripken III. But by the time we had Ryan, we changed our minds. We wanted Ryan to have his own name, and his own identity.

The year I married Kelly, 1987, my dad was named Oriole manager. Later that season, my brother Billy came up from the minors to play for the Orioles too. That was great.

But the Orioles were not doing well. We had lost too many experienced players. The team was going through changes and needed time to improve.

My dad was blamed. The very next season, after only six games, he was fired.

Billy and I continued to play our best for the team. We wanted to help it rebuild. Late in 1988, Dad came back as third base coach.

The Home Run Hitting Contest

The Orioles had good years and not so good years. So did I. For me, 1990 was tough. I had another major slump. And by then,

people had taken notice of my growing number of consecutive games.

Questions began to come up about my playing streak. People wondered if I was too tired to play. Some people thought I should take off a game or two.

I didn't want to think about the record. I wanted to concentrate on one game at a time. Slumps are a part of baseball. They happen. I knew I had to keep playing.

And I did break the slump. In 1991, I

hit 34 homers, with 114 runs batted in. By mid-season, I was hitting .348. That's a great batting average. I was leading the league. But I was on such a hot streak that I was a little disappointed with that number. I wanted a big round number like .350.

The night before the All-Star game, there was a home run hitting contest. I'm not known as a slugger, but I was fifth in the league in home runs, with 18. I qualified for the contest. I was excited.

I stepped into the box. The crowd cheered. I took a few pitches. Then I swung and hit a screaming line drive. That was one homer. Then came number two, then three, then four. At one point, I hit seven in a row. I was hitting balls as far as I've ever hit them. Teammates stood in the dugout, yelling and screaming.

I won the contest. I hit 12 homers on 22 swings. I was the first shortstop in history to do that.

The All-Star game was the next night. I hit a three-run homer. Everything really came together for me. I was in one sweet groove that day, and that year.

Of course, good streaks end, just like slumps. There were more tough years ahead. In 1992, Dad left the Orioles for good, and my brother Billy was let go from the team.

What else could I do? I kept playing. I played the best I could, in every game.

The Streak

I had been with the Orioles for twelve years. And for twelve years I met the challenges of each day. I didn't think about the future. I didn't think about breaking the consecutive games record.

Then came game number 2,000 in Minnesota. It was August 1994. There was a big salute to my streak. For the first time, I realized that the fans wanted me to break the record.

Why was everybody so excited? I didn't strike out 5,000 batters. I didn't hit more home runs than anybody else. What did I do? I showed up. I played as well as I could, and as often as I could.

I tried to understand the fans' feelings. They wanted to celebrate baseball. And they respected someone who showed up to do his job every day.

The fans probably felt the same way back in May 1939. That's when New York Yankee great Lou Gehrig ended his streak of 2,130

consecutive games. Lou Gehrig stopped playing because of a serious illness. But he was tough. And I feel honored to play the same game.

In 1995, excitement about the streak grew. Reporters wanted to interview me at almost every ballpark. My wife said I should try to enjoy the attention. I took her advice.

The press . . . the fans . . . the attention. It all seemed like a dream.

Then, on August 29, 1995, a huge banner was dropped on the Orioles' ball field wall. It read 2,123. There were only eight games to go. It suddenly seemed real.

Every time we played at home after that, a banner dropped. The feelings were so powerful! I was excited, but kind of embarrassed by all the attention too.

On September 5, we played a home game

against the Angels. When the first half of the
fifth inning ended, the game was official. I
had tied Lou Gehrig's record.

I was in the dugout when the banner
dropped to show the number 2,130. The ball
field exploded. Exploded! There were many
handshakes and hugs. I waved to the crowd
again and again.

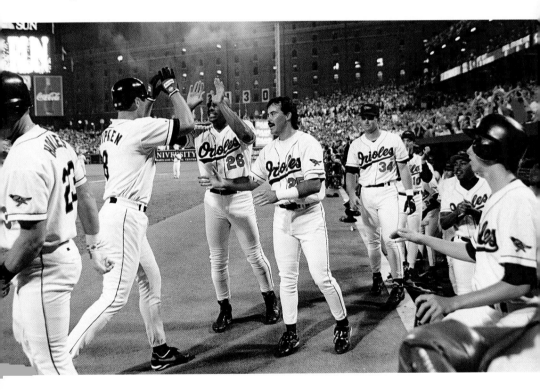

The next inning, I hit the ball over the left field wall. Home run! All of the Orioles were playing great baseball that night.

Then came September 6. This was the day I would break the record. It was another home game. It was also my daughter Rachel's first day in first grade. We were both having special days.

That night, Rachel and Ryan came to the game with Kelly and the rest of my family. My kids threw out the first balls.

In the bottom of the fourth inning, I stood at the plate. I saw the ball coming at me. It was a fastball right down the middle. I nailed that pitch. It was another homer!

One inning later, I officially broke the record. I was the new "Iron Man" of baseball. I stood in the field and tapped my heart. What more could I say? What more could I do?

Ten minutes later, the crowd was still going crazy. My teammates sent me out of the dugout, to take a lap around the bases.

I shook hands with my brother Billy, the

umpires, and the Angels. I wanted to shake hands with each one of the 46,000 people in the stands. But I couldn't reach that far.

Who won the game? The Orioles, 4–2!

Then came the ceremony. My teammates congratulated me. Gifts were presented. Then it was my turn at the microphone.

I thanked Mom, Dad, Kelly, Rachel, and Ryan. I thanked my old teammate Eddie Murray for his help. Then I talked about Lou Gehrig and what I love about baseball.

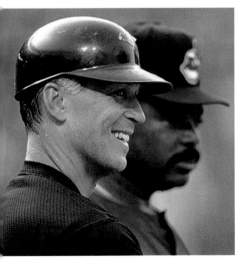

I said, "Whether your name is Gehrig or Ripken . . . or that of some youngster who picks up his bat or puts on his glove, you are challenged by the game of baseball to do your very best, day in and day out, and that's all I've ever tried to do."

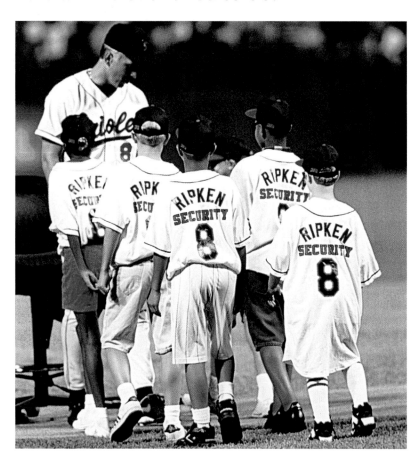

After the game, Kelly and I drove home.
We only said two sentences:

"Big night at the ballpark, huh?"

"Sure was."

In the 1996 season, the Orioles got into the playoffs. But we lost the American League championship to the Yankees.

In 1997, I played a new position—third

base. It felt like a new beginning. It was a new challenge. And I've always liked a challenge.

That year, I was almost laid up with an injury. But I took the challenge to keep playing. I ended up feeling fine, and we went on to another American League Championship series. This time, we lost to the Cleveland Indians. But the Orioles had a great year. We all felt proud.

On April 25,1998, I played in my 2,500th consecutive game. In July 1998 I played in my sixteenth All-Star game, in Denver, Colorado. On September 20, 1998, I took myself out of the lineup for the Orioles' last home game of the season. I thought the time was right. I had played 2,632 consecutive games.

What's next? What's my attitude for the future? It's the same as always. Try your best, keep playing, and see what happens!

Cal Ripken, Jr., Career Highlights

Born: Havre de Grace, Maryland, August 24, 1960
Height: 6 feet, 4 inches   **Weight**: 225 pounds
Team: Baltimore Orioles
Position: shortstop 1981–1996, third base 1997–present
Bats: Right   **Throws**: right
Nickname: The Iron Man

Some career statistics:

- Cal's playing streak began May 30, 1982. He broke the major league record for the most consecutive games played (2,130) on September 6, 1995, and set a new record by playing a total of 2,632 consecutive games.

- He set the record for the most home runs ever hit by a major league shortstop when he hit his 278th homer on July 15, 1993.

- He was selected Most Valuable Player in the American League in 1983 and 1991.

- He holds or shares 11 major league or American League fielding records.

- He has played in sixteen All-Star games.

- He played in the 1983 World Series, which the Orioles won.

- He was selected Rookie of the Year in the American League in 1982.

- He won the Golden Glove Award for fielding in 1991 and 1992.